How
Babies and Families
are Made

(There *is* more than one way!)

How Babies and Families are Made

(There *is* more than one way!)

by Patricia Schaffer

illustrated by Suzanne Corbett

TABOR SARAH BOOKS

Berkeley, California

Fourth printing 1996
Third printing 1993
Second printing 1991

Printed in the United States of America

Library of Congress Cataloging-in-Publication Data

Schaffer, Patricia, 1950–
    How Families and Babies are Made

    Summary: Surveys the different ways in which children are conceived, develop, are born, and become parts of families, examining special situations such as artificial insemination, cesarean births, and families with adopted children or stepchildren.
    1. Sex instruction for children. [1. Sex instruction for children. 2. Family]
I. Corbett, Suzanne, ill.   II. Title.
HQ53.S3   1988   306.8'5   86-23087
ISBN 0-935079-17-3

Layout: Rachel Blau
Typesetting: *turnaround,* Berkeley

For Akiva Daniel, Micah Jody, and Rebecca Yang-Hee

PREFACE

When a child asks about where babies come from, it is almost necessary to have a book with pictures that help you to explain. It is also helpful to have the words and information that make teaching possible. In this book you will find detailed information about anatomy. You may wish to read these pages to yourself and then tell the child about it in your own words while referring to the illustrations. Children are not expected to remember all the "big words" but should know such words exist. It is important for children to know the proper terms for more familiar body parts, even if you have not previously used them in your home.

Not all children are conceived by sexual intercourse. To teach that they are is simply untrue. It is estimated that 25,000 babies were conceived by artificial insemination in this country in 1985. Worldwide over 2,000 babies have been born to women who have gone through in vitro fertilization. In the United States alone there are 150 clinics performing this procedure. One can only guess what forms of conception will be possible by the time today's children are grown.

The composition of American families has changed rapidly over the last 15 years. Of children born in 1986 it is predicted that most will live with a single parent at some time before reaching the age of 18. Eventually, the combined number of stepparent and single parent families will surpass the number of "traditional" two-parent families. Many "traditional" families include adopted children. In 1983 over 50,000 children were adopted in this country. It is important for children to know that all kinds of families exist and are of equal value.

As you will see, I have tried to make all children feel included in the pages of this book. I hope you feel welcome as well.

Patricia Schaffer
Berkeley, California

Rachel and Michael are friends. Some things about them are the same and some things are different. They play baseball on the same team. In good weather they ride their bicycles together to school. They both have brown hair and brown eyes.

Michael's skin is darker than Rachel's. Rachel's hair is straighter than Michael's. Rachel likes the feel of the wind in her hair. Michael always wears his baseball cap.

Michael and Rachel are the same as you in some ways. In other ways they are different from you.

What do you think a family is?

A family is people caring about each other. They can be people you live with or who do not live with you. There can be one or more children in a family. There can be one or more parents.

Rachel's family includes her mother, father, and a younger sister.

Families can change over time. As babies or children are added, a family grows. When people marry, families can join together.

Michael has a mother, father and stepmother. He has two homes and spends time in both of them.

A family can be grandparents raising their grandchildren. Some families have only adults in them. Other families include parents, children and special friends.

You probably know other kinds of families.
Perhaps your friends or neighbors have families
that are not like yours.

Who is in your family?

Michael and Rachel wonder about when they were babies. They want to know how babies are born. Maybe you too want to know.

We all began with the joining of a cell from a woman's body and a cell from a man's body. Each of us grew inside a woman's body. Each of us came out of a woman as a newborn baby.

To find out how Michael, Rachel and you began, you must know some things about the bodies of women and men.

Here is a picture of the inside parts of women that are needed to make a baby. There are two **ovaries** with thousands of tiny **ova** in them. Another word for ova is "eggs," but these "eggs" have no shell. A single egg is called an **ovum**. It is smaller than the period at the end of this sentence.

Near each ovary is an end of a **fallopian tube**. The other end of each tube is attached to the **uterus**. A fallopian tube is as narrow as a hair. The bottom end of the uterus is called the **cervix**. From the cervix the **vagina** leads outside of the body to the **vulva**.

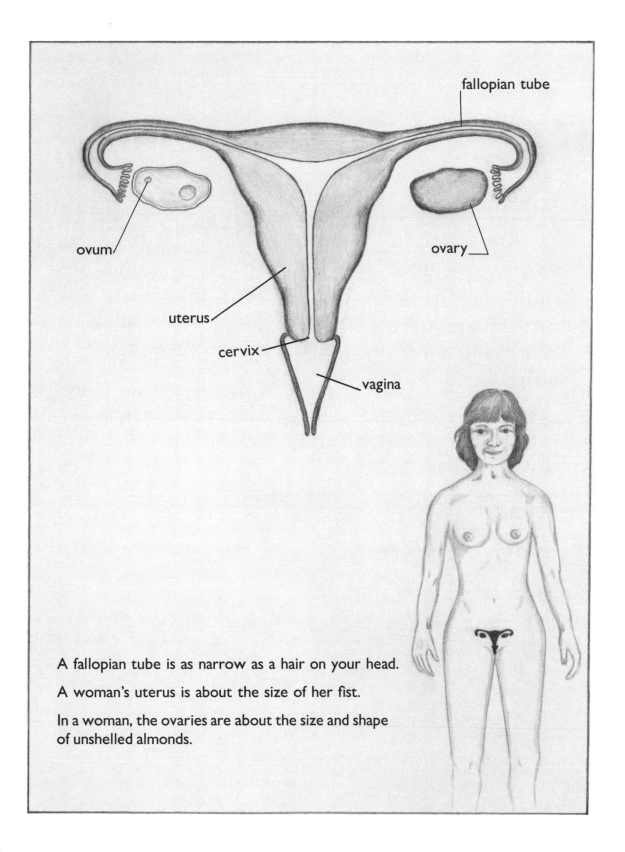

fallopian tube

ovary

ovum

uterus

cervix

vagina

A fallopian tube is as narrow as a hair on your head.

A woman's uterus is about the size of her fist.

In a woman, the ovaries are about the size and shape of unshelled almonds.

When you look at the picture of Rachel, you can see the outer part of her vulva between her legs. Her mother has hair covering the outer part of her vulva. What you cannot see are the opening to the vagina, the **urethra** and the **clitoris**. They are hidden by the sides of the vulva. Urine, or pee, comes out of the urethra. The clitoris is a sensitive female sex organ.

Rachel's body will grow to look more like her mother's as she gets older. Her body cannot work to make a baby yet.

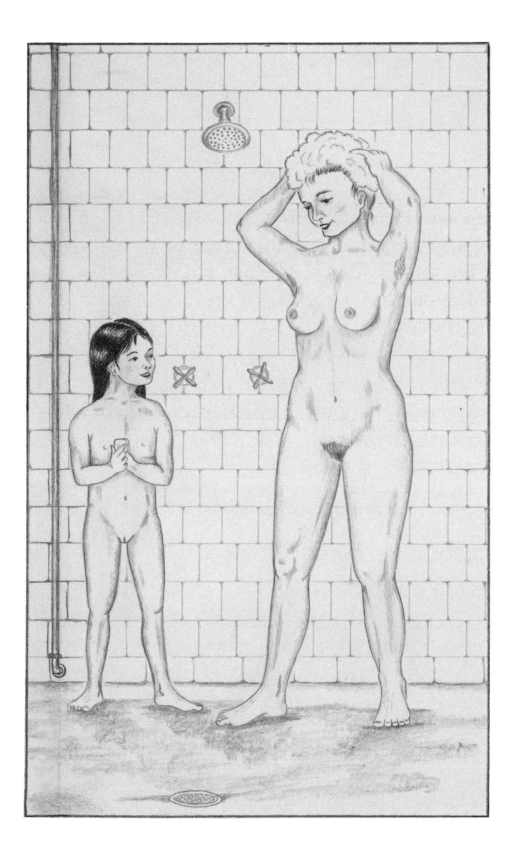

Here is a picture of Michael and his father. In between their legs, attached to the lower part of their bodies, they each have a **penis**. Behind the penis is a pouch of skin called the **scrotum**. In the scrotum are the **testes**. They feel like two small balls. It is in these small balls, the testes, that **sperm** are made. Sperm are very, very small. You cannot see them without a microscope. In an adult male a hundred million sperm may be produced each day.

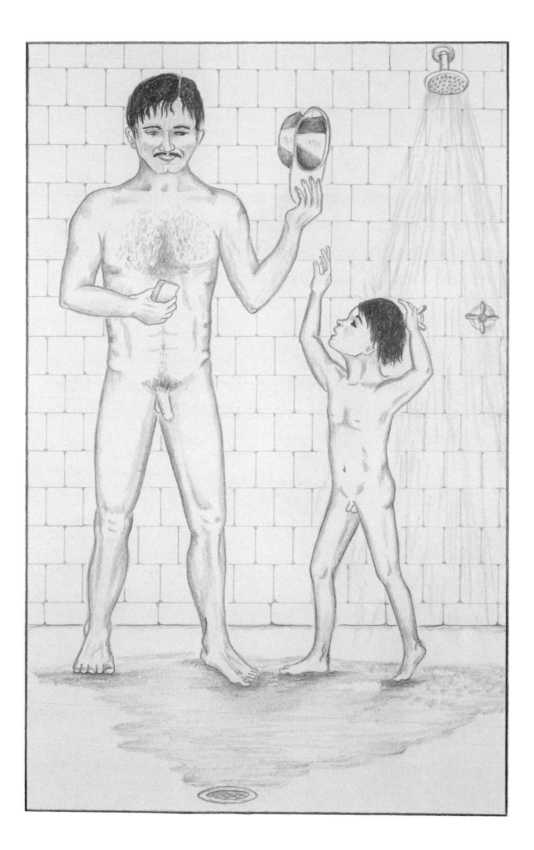

The sperm leave the testes through tubes called the **vas deferens**. They are mixed with a liquid called **semen** and stored in pouches inside the body called **seminal vesicles**.

Both semen and urine come out of the penis — but never at the same time.

Michael's body will grow to look more like his father's body as he becomes older. Michael's testes do not produce sperm yet.

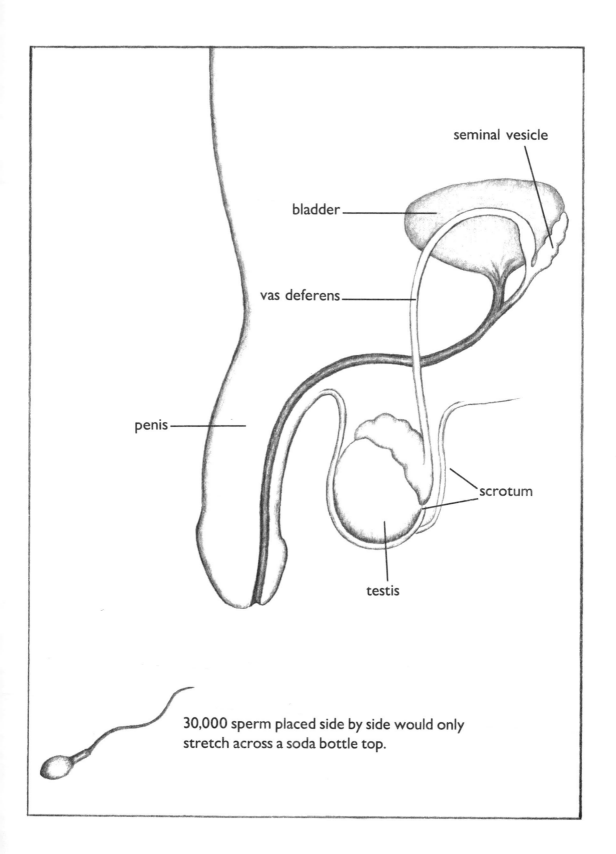

seminal vesicle

bladder

vas deferens

penis

scrotum

testis

30,000 sperm placed side by side would only stretch across a soda bottle top.

Now you know the parts of the body needed to begin to make a baby. How do these parts work together?

The most common way to start a baby is called **sexual intercourse**. A woman and a man feel like getting very close to one another. They hug and kiss. They touch each other's bodies because it feels good. They decide to get extra close by putting the man's penis into the woman's vagina.

The cloudy-colored liquid called semen comes out of the man's penis. The sperm travel up the woman's vagina. They go through her cervix and uterus into her fallopian tubes. If an ovum (egg) has been released by the ovary, it moves through the fallopian tube. If it joins with a sperm, we say it has become **fertilized**. The new cell, the combination of ovum and sperm, may develop into a baby. People do not make a baby every time they have intercourse.

This is how Michael's parents made him.

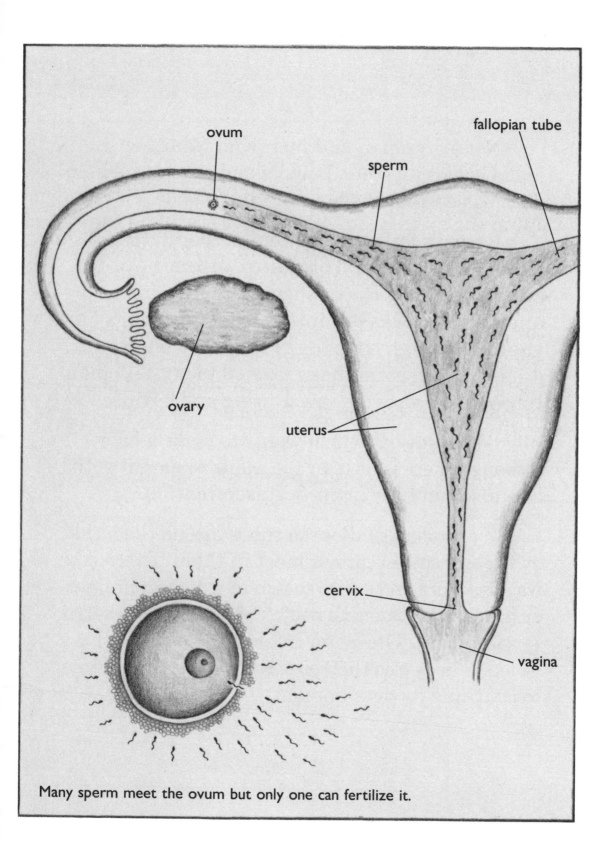

ovum

fallopian tube

sperm

ovary

uterus

cervix

vagina

Many sperm meet the ovum but only one can fertilize it.

Not all women and men who want to can make babies together. Doctors and nurses can help with some problems but not all.

Rachel's father cannot make sperm. Her mother had **artificial** or **donor insemination**, and that is how Rachel began. Sperm from another man was put into Rachel's mother's vagina through a syringe similar to an eye dropper. The sperm then traveled to her fallopian tubes where an ovum was waiting and fertilized it.

Sometimes a woman wants to make a baby although there is no man she wants to have it with. She also can have artificial insemination.

If a woman's fallopian tubes are blocked, the ovum and sperm cannot meet in them. There is a way for ovum and sperm to join in a glass container outside of the woman's body. This is called **in vitro fertilization**. The ovum is fertilized outside the woman's body and then put into the woman's uterus to continue its development.

Five or six days after fertilization, the ball of cells has moved into the woman's uterus. In the uterus the cells continue to divide, gradually developing into a baby. The uterus is a safe and warm place for a baby to be until it is born. Most babies stay in the uterus for about nine months.

A baby begins as one cell, the fertilized ovum. This cell divides into two cells, then the two become four, then eight and so on. When a baby is born, it is made up of more than 200 billion cells!

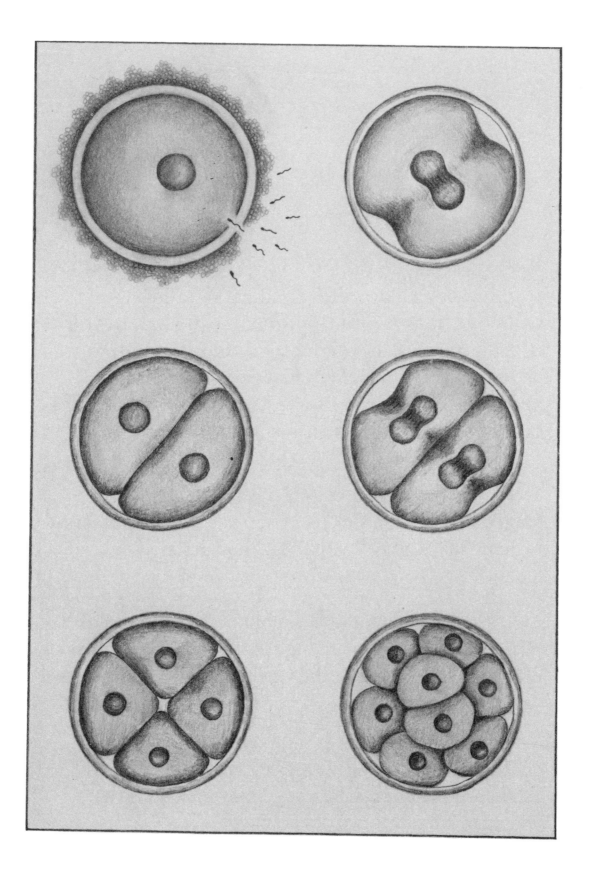

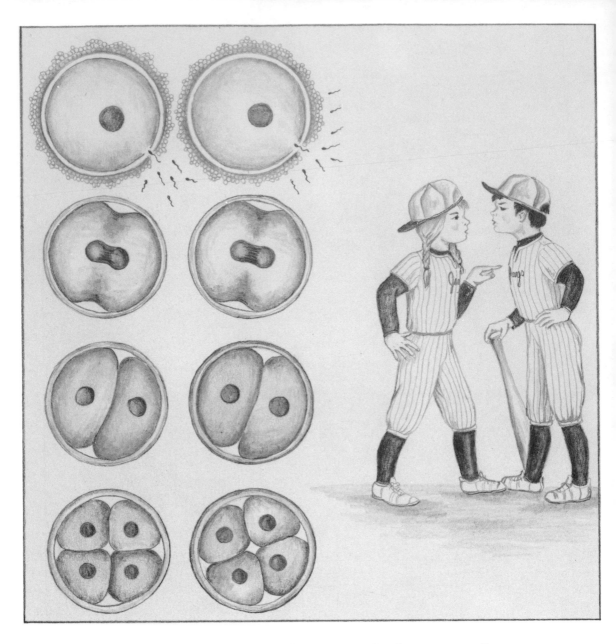

Sometimes more than one baby is made at a time. Two babies born together are called **twins**. More rarely, three babies, **triplets**, or even more are born together.

If two or more ova (eggs) are fertilized, the babies are as different as any children made by the same woman and man. They can be girls, boys, or one or more of each.

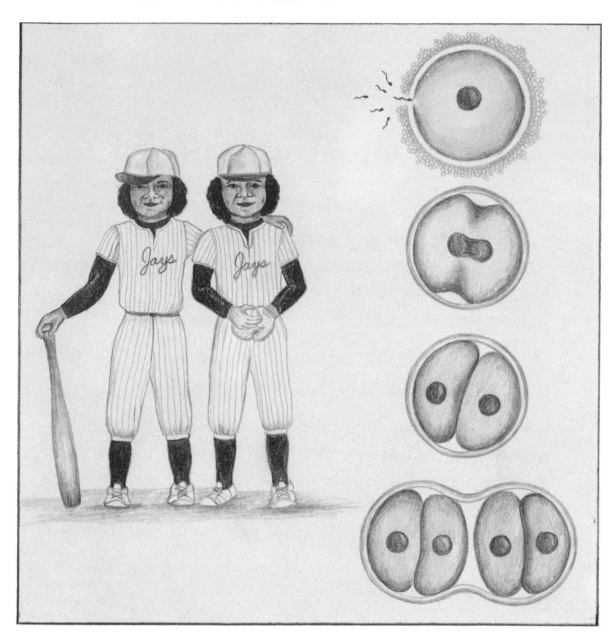

When a single fertilized ovum divides into two or more completely separate balls of cells, identical babies develop. These babies grow to look exactly alike. They are all girls or all boys.

Do you know any twins? Eli and Jessica and Tiffany and Keisha are on the same baseball team as Rachel and Michael.

When a woman has a baby growing in her, we say she is **pregnant.** As the baby grows larger, the woman's uterus also grows. Have you ever seen a pregnant woman?

A pregnant woman's breasts grow bigger. They are getting ready to make milk for her baby.

After she as been pregnant for a few months, a woman may have special tests to find out if her baby is healthy. She can also find out the sex of her baby, if it is a girl or a boy. These tests are given for medical reasons, not just to find out the sex of the baby.

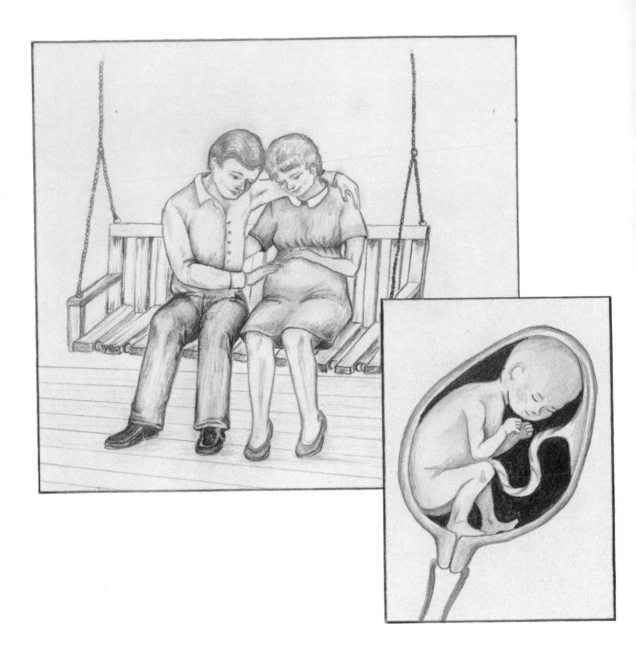

At first the baby in the uterus is very, very small. After three months it is about 2¾ inches long [——————————————]. Already it can move its tiny arms and legs.

After five months, Rachel's father could feel her kicking by putting his hand on her mother's tummy.

By the end of the seventh month in the uterus, a baby is completely formed. During the next two months it continues to grow bigger and stronger so it can live outside of the uterus.

Babies can see and hear while in the uterus though it is dark and sounds are muffled. Michael's mom could feel when he hiccupped. Some babies suck their thumbs before they are born.

Sometimes things do not go right. The baby comes out early because it has died. This is called a **miscarriage**. Other times a baby may die at birth or soon after it is born. Everyone who was excited about the new baby coming is very sad. After she has had time to rest and feel better, a woman may decide to try to get pregnant again. This time the baby will probably be fine.

Babies are usually born in a hospital or at home. Do you know where you were born?

Many women prefer to go to the hospital to have their babies in case they or their baby need emergency help. Michael was born in a hospital.

Rachel's mother wanted to have her baby at home because she felt more comfortable there.

Doctors and midwives know how to help women with the birth of their babies.

When it is time for her baby to be born, a woman will feel some pain. This is because the muscles of her uterus are beginning to contract, to push and pull. They work to open the cervix. The woman is said to be **in labor**. Other muscles then push the baby out through the woman's vagina. Her vagina stretches very wide as the baby passes. It then shrinks right back. Labor can last only a few hours or as long as a couple of days.

Rachel's mother was in labor for 14 hours.

There are many reasons why a baby may not be born through a women's vagina. Sometimes the baby is in a position that makes it hard for it to come out. Perhaps the woman's cervix will not open. These babies are born by an operation called **cesarean section**.

This is how Michael was born. His mother was given special medicines so she did not feel any pain. The doctor cut through her skin and through her uterus and lifted Michael out. The opening was sewn up and healed in a short time.

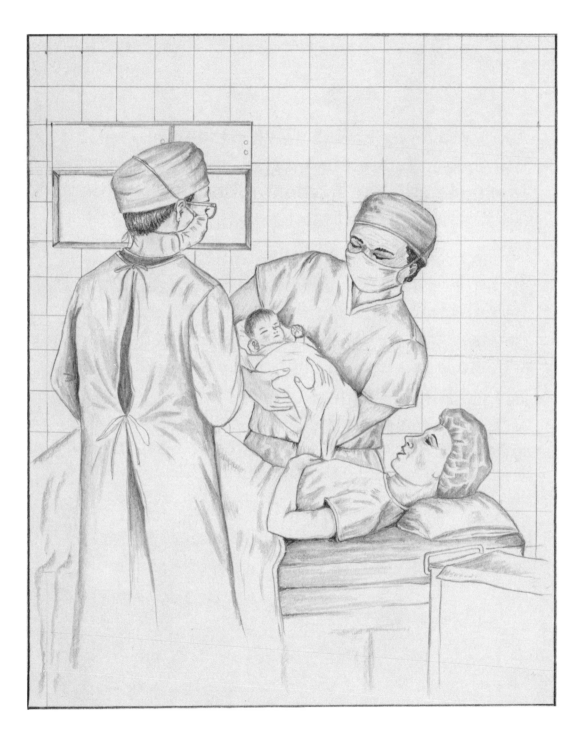

As soon as Rachel and Michael were born they began to breathe on their own. Rachel cried. Michael didn't cry. Rachel wanted to look around. Michael wanted to take a nap.

After a baby is born the **umbilical cord**, through which the baby received oxygen and nourishment while in the uterus, is no longer needed. The cord is clamped and cut by the person who helped with the birth. This does not hurt the baby. A little piece of the cord is left. In less than two weeks the piece usually falls off. Do you know where your umbilical cord was attached to you? Now your belly button is there!

Not all babies are developed enough when they are born to live outside of the uterus without extra medical help. Some are born too soon and some are too little. These babies are called **premature**. They are placed in special baby beds called **incubators**. There they are kept warm and may be given extra oxygen and nourishment.

Some babies must spend weeks or even months in the hospital. It is a happy day when they are strong enough to go home.

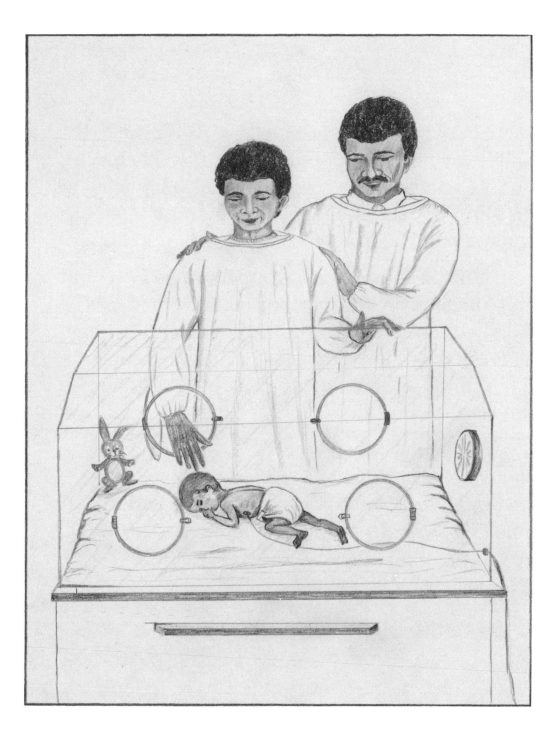

Some babies are born with a **disability**. A baby may need an operation on her or his lip, heart or another part of the body. A baby may be blind or deaf. Maybe what is wrong with the baby can be fixed and maybe not.

A disability may make a person look, act or move differently from most people. Sometimes a baby will not grow to be able to learn as fast or as much as others. Even though people seem different on the outside, they share the same kinds of feelings inside.

Did you need some extra special care when you were born? Michael's friend Danny moves in a wheelchair. He needs to wear glasses with thick lenses in order to see his school work.

There are several ways for children to become part of a family. They can be born into it. They can join a family through marriage. They can be adopted into it.

Some families are a mix of different relationships. There may be biological, adopted and stepchildren all in the same family.

If children live with the mother and father who made them, they live with their **biological family**. Everyone has a biological family but not everyone knows or lives with that family.

If a parent is divorced or widowed and remarries, the children have **stepparents**. A mother's new husband is a **stepfather**. If a father has a new wife, she is a **stepmother**. A single parent may marry, and that new partner will be a stepparent. There may be stepsisters and stepbrothers, too.

When children share only one biological parent they are called **half brothers** or **half sisters**. If Michael's father and stepmother have a baby girl, that child will be his half sister.

When a child joins a family in which the parents did not make her or him, we say the child has been **adopted.** The woman who gave birth to the child is the child's **birthmother**. The man whose sperm fertilized the ovum is called the child's **birthfather.**

Sometimes **birthparents** are not able to take care of a child. They may not feel old enough to be parents. They may not have the support they need to raise a child. The birthparents may decide to make an adoption plan for their child so the child will have a family that is ready to take care of her or him. Sometimes a child lives in a foster home or an orphanage and is taken care of there until it is time to join a new family.

A woman and a man may adopt a child because they cannot make any children together and want to be parents. Other people may already be parents and want to have more children in their family. A stepparent may adopt a stepchild. Sometimes a single person can adopt. Babies as well as older children can be adopted.

Some children are adopted in the same country they are born in; others come from different countries. Rachel's cousin Miriam was adopted. She was born in Korea. Miriam lived in a foster home for three months before joining Rachel's aunt and uncle.

Rachel and Michael continued to grow after they were born. They are still growing. They are learning about the world and the people in it. You are growing every day and learning new things, too.

There are things about you that are different from Michael, Rachel and everyone else. There are other things that are the same. You too began from the joining of an ovum and a sperm. You grew in a woman's uterus. You were born as a little baby.

Rachel and Michael are part of the human family. You are too.

How Babies and Families Are Made
(There *is* more than one way!)

1-4 Copies $7.95 each, 5 or more copies 20% discount

Books ordered_____x $7.95   = _____

-20% discount for 5 or more copies   = _____

CA residents add 7% sales tax   = _____

Shipping book rate $1.75 first copy   = _____

each additional copy $.75   = _____

TOTAL ENCLOSED   = _____

Ship to:_____

_____

_____Zip_____

Make check payable to:

Tabor Sarah Books
3345 Stockton Place
Palo Alto, CA 94303

(415)494-7846